easy fairisle knits

14 small projects in Rowan *Felted Tweed*

Martin Storey

Photography by Steven Wooster

R O W A N

Easy Fairisle Knits
First published in 2014 by
Rowan Yarns/Coats Crafts UK
Green Lane Mill
Holmfirth
HD9 2DX

Created and produced by
Berry & Co (Publishing) Ltd
47 Crewys Road
Childs Hill
London NW2 2AU
www.berrypublishing.co.uk

Designer: Anne Wilson
Editor: Katie Hardwicke
Pattern writer (and knitting): Penny Hill
Pattern checker: Jill Gray
Charts: Anne Wilson
Stylist: Susan Berry
Special photography (pages 5, 62-3, 64
and back cover): Hazel Young

British Library Cataloguing in Publication Data
A catalogue record of this book is available
from the British Library.

ISBN 978-1-907544-87-3
Printed in China

contents

introduction

When I was asked to create the designs for a book of patterns that made
Fairisle both simple and contemporary, I jumped at the chance, because
I love to work with colour and particularly enjoy the intricate but
subtle effect you get when knitting with two colours in a row. In fact,
I had fairly recently returned from a wonderful workshop in the Shetland
Islands, which gave me lots of inspiration for this book.

Lots of people love the look of Fairisle patterns but assume it will be
difficult to knit them. That is certainly true of some of the exquisite
traditional Fairisle sweaters with lots of colour changes, but even a
novice knitter would not find the patterns in this book hard to knit for
three reasons: firstly the designs I have included are generally small;
secondly the majority have no shaping (which can be harder to work in
Fairisle); and thirdly they only employ two colours in a row, which is
not hard to handle even for a novice knitter.

I have included quite a few cushions in the book, in part because I think
the Fairisle patterns are a great addition to an otherwise plain sofa or
chair, and also because once you get into the groove, they are very easy
to work. You can then put several different patterned cushions together
to great effect. The scarves are similarly easy to knit. Even the bag is
not difficult because the Fairisle pattern is worked on a straight piece
of knitting.

The socks, hats and slipover are a little more complicated but not much,
because the Fairisle element is kept pretty simple and there is very
little shaping to do at the points when the more complicated Fairisle
pattern is involved. As an extra bit of fun, I have included a Nordic
tree design for a cushion, throw and garland. The latter could be knitted
quite easily even by a child!

I hope you have as much fun knitting the designs as I did creating them.

little circles scarf

little circles cushion

paper dolls cushion

simple
spots
cushion

13

tree and ripple bag

kitten and stripe scarf

waves slipover

19

plaid and diamond beanie

plaid
and
diamond
socks

soft stripes gloves...

...and soft stripes beret

nordic throw

nordic cushion

nordic garland

little circles scarf

FINISHED SIZE
One size: 15cm/6in wide by 110cm/43¼in long

YARN
Rowan *Felted Tweed DK*
3 x 50g balls in Celadon 184 (A)
1 x 50g ball in each of Tawny 186 (B) and Mineral (C)

NEEDLES
Pair each of 3.25mm (US 3) and 3.75mm (US 5) needles

TENSION
23 sts and 32 rows to 10cm/4in square over St st using 3.75mm (US 5) needles, or size to obtain correct tension.

ABBREVIATIONS
See page 63.

NOTE
When working from Chart, odd numbered rows are knit rows and read from right to left. Even numbered rows are purl rows and read from left to right.
Use the Fairisle method, strand the yarn not in use across the wrong side of work, weaving them under and over the working yarn every 3 or 4 sts.

TO MAKE (make 2 pieces)
Using 3.75mm (US 5) needles and A, cast on 72 sts.
Beg with a k row, work in St st and patt from Chart.
Row 1 Using A, k to end.
Row 2 Using A, p to end.
Row 3 Work one st before patt rep, [work across 5-st patt rep] 14 times, work one st after patt rep.
Row 4 Work one st before patt rep, [work across 5-st patt rep] 14 times, work one st after patt rep.
Rows 3 and 4 set the Chart.
Work in patt to end of row 12.
Rows 13 to 23 Rep rows 3 to 12 once, and row 3 again.
Row 24 Using A, p to end.
Row 25 Using A, k to end.
Row 26 P2A, P[1C, 3A] to last 2 sts, 1C, 1A.
Row 27 Using A, k to end.
Row 28 Using A, p to end.
Row 29 K[3A, 1C] to end.
Rows 24 to 29 form the spot patt.
Cont in spot patt until piece measures 55cm/21¾in, ending with a plain row.
Leave sts on a spare needle.

TO MAKE UP
With needles pointing in the same direction, right sides together, using A cast off the sts of both pieces together.
Join row ends of scarf together.
With seam running down centre of scarf, using 3.25mm (US 3) needles and C, working through both thicknesses pick up and k24 sts along one short end.
K 2 rows.
Cast off.
Work other end to match.

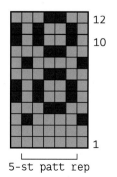

5-st patt rep

KEY

Celadon 184 (A)
Tawny 186 (B)

little circles cushion

FINISHED SIZE
38cm/15in by 38cm/15in to fit a 40cm/16in square cushion pad

YARN
Rowan *Felted Tweed DK*
3 x 50g balls in Celadon 184 (A)
1 x 50g ball in each of Tawny 186 (B) and Mineral (C)

NEEDLES
Pair of 3.75mm (US 5) knitting needles

EXTRAS
40cm/16in cushion pad

TENSION
23 sts and 32 rows to 10cm/4in square over St st using 3.75mm (US 5) needles, or size to obtain correct tension.

ABBREVIATIONS
See page 63.

NOTE
When working from Chart, odd numbered rows are knit rows and read from right to left. Even numbered rows are purl rows and read from left to right.
Use the Fairisle method, strand the yarn not in use across the wrong side of work weaving them under and over the working yarn every 3 or 4 sts.

FRONT
Using 3.75mm (US 5) needles and A, cast on 92 sts.
Row 1 Using A, k to end.
Row 2 P2A, P[1C, 3A] to last 2 sts, 1C, 1A.
Row 3 Using A, k to end.
Row 4 Using A, p to end.
Row 5 K[3A, 1C] to end.
Row 6 Using A, p to end.

Rows 1 to 6 form the spot patt.
Work a further 43 rows, ending with row 1.
Work in St st and patt from Chart on page 34.
Row 50 Work one st before patt rep, [work across 5-st patt rep] 18 times, work one st after patt rep.
Row 51 Work one st before patt rep, [work across 5-st patt rep] 18 times, work one st after patt rep.
Rows 50 and 51 set the Chart.
Work in patt to end of row 12, then rows 3 to 7.
Rows 61 to 71 Rep rows 50 to 60 once, and row 50 again.
Rows 72 to 120 Rep rows 1 to 6 eight times and row 1 again.
Using A, cast off.

BACK
Using 3.75mm (US 5) needles and A, cast on 92 sts.
Row 1 Using A, k to end.
Row 2 P2A, P[1C, 3A] to last 2 sts, 1C, 1A.
Row 3 Using A, k to end.
Row 4 Using A, p to end.
Row 5 K[3A, 1C] to end.
Row 6 Using A, p to end.
Rows 1 to 6 form the spot patt.
Rows 7 to 120 Rep rows 1 to 6 nineteen times more.
Using A, cast off.

TO MAKE UP
With right sides together, sew back to front along three sides. Insert cushion pad, join rem side.

paper dolls cushion

FINISHED SIZE
38cm/15in by 38cm/15in to fit a 40cm/16in square cushion pad

YARN
Rowan *Felted Tweed DK*
2 x 50g balls in Duck Egg 173 (A)
1 x 50g ball in each of Tawny 186 (B), Mineral 181 (C) and Hedgerow 187 (D)

NEEDLES
Pair of 3.75mm (US 5) knitting needles

EXTRAS
40cm/16in cushion pad

TENSION
23 sts and 32 rows to 10cm/4in square over St st using 3.75mm (US 5) needles. 24 sts and 32 rows to 10cm/4in square over patt St St using 3.75mm (US 5) needles, or size to obtain correct tension.

ABBREVIATIONS
See page 63.

NOTE
When working from Chart, odd numbered rows are knit rows and read from right to left. Even numbered rows are purl rows and read from left to right.
Use the Fairisle method, strand the yarn not in use across the wrong side of work weaving them under and over the working yarn every 3 or 4 sts.

FRONT
Using 3.75mm (US 5) needles and A, cast on 91 sts.
P 1 row.
Work in patt from Chart A.
Row 1 (RS) Work 2 sts before patt rep, then [work across 8-st patt rep] 11 times, work one st after patt rep.
Row 2 Work one st before patt rep, [work across 8-st patt rep] 11 times, work 2 sts after patt rep.
These 2 rows set Chart A.
Work in patt to end of row 23.
Work in patt from Chart B.
Row 1 (WS) [Work across 7-st patt rep] 13 times.
Row 2 [Work across 7-st patt rep] 13 times.
These 2 rows set Chart B.
Work in patt to end of row 9.
These 32 rows set the patt.
Work a further 87 rows, ending row 23 of Chart A.
Cast off.

BACK
Using 3.75mm (US 5) needles and A, cast on 87 sts.
P 1 row.
Beg with a k row, work in St st and stripes of:
1 row A, 3 rows C, [3 rows A, 1 row B] 3 times, 3 rows A, = 15 rows.
3 rows C **, [1 row A, 2 rows D] 3 times, 1 row A, = 10 rows.
These 32 rows form the stripe sequence, see photograph on page 37, left.
Work a further 86 rows, ending row at **.
Work 1 row A.
Cast off.

TO MAKE UP
With right sides together, sew back to front along three sides. Insert cushion pad, join rem side.

CHART A

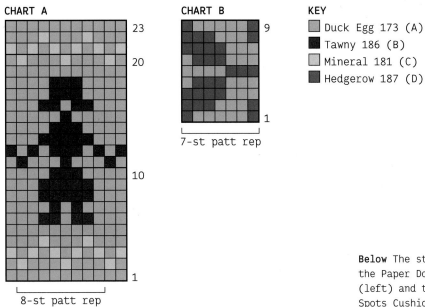

23

20

10

1

8-st patt rep

CHART B

9

1

7-st patt rep

KEY
- Duck Egg 173 (A)
- Tawny 186 (B)
- Mineral 181 (C)
- Hedgerow 187 (D)

Below The striped backs of the Paper Dolls Cushion (left) and the Simple Spots Cushion (right).

simple spots cushion

FINISHED SIZE
38cm/15in by 38cm/15in to fit a 40cm/16in square cushion pad

YARN
Rowan *Felted Tweed DK*
1 x 50g ball in each of Frozen 185 (A), Cinnamon 175 (B), Avocado 161 (C), Tawny 186 (D) and Maritime 167 (E)

NEEDLES
Pair of 3.75mm (US 5) knitting needles

EXTRAS
40cm/16in cushion pad

TENSION
23 sts and 32 rows to 10cm/4in square over St st using 3.75mm (US 5) needles. 24 sts and 32 rows to 10cm/4in square over patt using 3.75mm (US 5) needles, or size to obtain correct tension.

ABBREVIATIONS
See page 63.

NOTE
When working from Chart, odd numbered rows are knit rows and read from right to left. Even numbered rows are purl rows and read from left to right.
Use the Fairisle method, strand the yarn not in use across the wrong side of work weaving them under and over the working yarn every 3 or 4 sts.

FRONT
Using 3.75mm (US 5) needles and A, cast on 91 sts.
P 1 row.
Work in patt.
Row 1 Work 3 sts before patt rep, [work across 8-st patt rep] 11 times.
Row 2 [Work across 8-st patt rep] 11

times, work 3 sts after patt rep.
These 2 rows set the Chart.
Work in patt to end of row 20.
These 20 rows set the patt.
Work a further 100 rows.
Row 121 Using A, k to end.
Cast off.

BACK
Using 3.75mm (US 5) needles and A, cast on 87 sts.
P 1 row.
Beg with a k row, work in St st and stripes of [5 rows, B, 5 rows E, 5 rows D, 5 rows C] 6 times, see photograph on page 37, right.
Row 121 Using A, k to end.
Cast off.

TO MAKE UP
With right sides together, sew back to front along three sides. Insert cushion pad, join rem side.

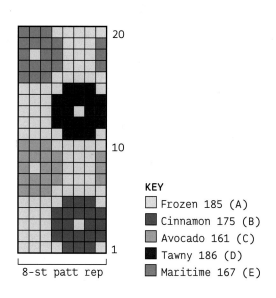

KEY
☐ Frozen 185 (A)
■ Cinnamon 175 (B)
☐ Avocado 161 (C)
■ Tawny 186 (D)
■ Maritime 167 (E)

8-st patt rep

tree and ripple bag

FINISHED SIZE
Approx 30cm/11¾in wide by 32cm/12½in deep

YARN
Rowan *Felted Tweed DK*
2 x 50g balls in Clay 177 (A)
1 x 50g ball in each of Gilt 160 (B),
Celadon 184 (C), Damask 182 (D) and
Maritime 167 (E)

NEEDLES
Pair each of 3.25mm (US 3) and 3.75mm (US
5) knitting needles
3.25mm (US 3) circular needle
Stitch holders

EXTRAS
100cm/39in of 2.5cm/1in wide petersham
ribbon

TENSION
26 sts and 26 rows to 10cm/4in square
patterned St st using 3.75mm (US 5)
needles, or size to obtain correct
tension.

ABBREVIATIONS
See page 63.

NOTE
When working from Chart, odd numbered
rows are knit rows and read from right
to left. Even numbered rows are purl rows
and read from left to right.
Use the Fairisle method, strand the yarn
not in use across the wrong side of work
weaving them under and over the working
yarn every 3 or 4 sts.

BAG
BACK AND FRONT (alike)
Using 3.75mm (US 5) needles and A, cast on
73 sts.
Work in patt from Chart A.
Row 1 [Work across 12-st patt rep] 6
times, then work last st of Chart.
Row 2 Work first st of Chart, then [work
across 12-st patt rep] 6 times.
These 2 rows set the Chart.
Work in patt from Chart to end of row 20.
Next row K to end, inc one st at centre of
row. *74 sts.*
Work in patt from Chart B.
Row 1 Work one st before patt rep, [work
across 6-st patt rep] 12 times, then work
one st after patt.
Row 2 Work one st before patt rep, [work
across 6-st patt rep] 12 times, then work
one st after patt.
These 2 rows set the Chart.
Cont in patt to end of row 16, then rep
rows 1 to 16 until piece measures approx
31cm/12in, ending on a p row in A.
Leave these sts on a holder.

GUSSET (make 2)
Using 3.75mm (US 5) needles and A, cast on
19 sts.
Beg with a k row, work in St st until
piece fits from halfway across cast-on
edge, ending with a p row, inc one st at
end of last row.
Mark each end of last row with a coloured
thread.
Work in patt from Chart C.
Row 1 K2A, work across 15 sts of Chart C,
k2A.
Row 2 P2A, work across 15 sts of Chart C,
p2A.
These 2 rows set the Chart.
Work in patt from Chart to end of row 20.
Next row K to end, inc one st at centre of
row. *20 sts.*

Work in patt from Chart B.
Row 1 Work one st before patt rep, [work across 6-st patt rep] 3 times, then work one st after patt.
Row 2 Work one st before patt rep, [work across 6-st patt rep] 3 times, then work one st after patt.
These 2 rows set the Chart.
Cont in patt to end of row 16, then rep rows 1 to 16 until piece measures approx 31cm/12in from coloured threads, ending on a p row in A.
Leave these sts on a holder.

HANDLES (make 2)
Using 3.75mm (US 5) needles and A, cast on 21 sts.
Next row K5, sl 1pw, k9, sl 1pw, k5.

KEY
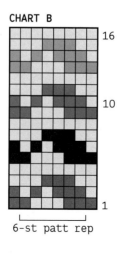
Clay 177 (A)
Gilt 160 (B)
Celadon 184 (C)
Damask 182 (D)
Maritime 167 (E)

Next row P to end.
Rep the last 2 rows 64 times more.
Cast off.

LINING
BACK AND FRONT (both alike)
Using 3.25mm (US 3) needles and A, cast on 74 sts.
Beg with a k row, cont in St st and stripes as folls:
[2 rows A, 2 rows C] 5 times, then [1 row A, 3 rows B, 1 row A, 3 rows D, 1 row A, 3 rows E, 1 row A, 3 rows C] until work measures same as main piece.
Leave these sts on a holder.

GUSSET (make 2)
Using 3.25mm (US 3) needles and A, cast on 18 sts.
Beg with a k row, work in St st until piece fits from halfway across cast-on edge, ending with a p row.
Beg with a k row, work in St st and stripes as folls:
[2 rows A, 2 rows C] 5 times, then [1 row A, 3 rows B, 1 row A, 3 rows D, 1 row A, 3 rows E, 1 row A, 3 rows C] until same

CHART A
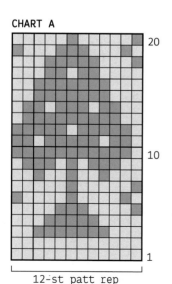
12-st patt rep

CHART B
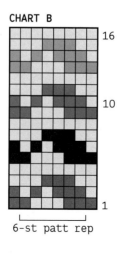
6-st patt rep

CHART C
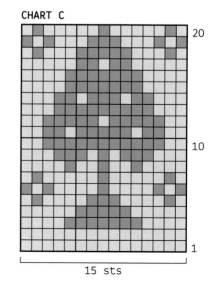
15 sts

number of 'stripes' have
been worked as on main
piece.
Leave these sts on a
holder.

TO MAKE UP

Join cast-on edges of
gussets.
Sew row ends of gusset
to row ends and cast-on
edges of back and front.
Make up lining in same
way. With wrong sides
together, place lining
inside bag.
Using 3.25mm (US 3)
needles and A, k together
one st from bag and one
st from lining all round
top edge.
Work in rounds.
Next round P to end.
Next round K to end.
Rep the last 2 rounds
twice more.
Cast off pwise.

Cut petersham ribbon in
half. Place petersham
ribbon along centre of
wrong side of handle and
slip stitch in place
along knitted slipped
sts. Bring row ends of
handle together encasing
petersham ribbon and sew
row ends together to
form seam. Sew handles
in place to inside of
bag. For extra stiffness
in bottom of bag, cut a
piece of cardboard to fit
along the base.

kitten and stripe scarf

FINISHED SIZE
One size: approx 11cm/4¾in wide by
190cm/75in long

YARN
Rowan *Felted Tweed DK*
2 x 50g balls in Scree 165 (A)
1 x 50g ball in each of Bilberry 151
(B), Avocado 161 (C), Ginger 154 (D) and
Watery 152 (E)

NEEDLES
Pair each of 3.25mm (US 3) and 3.75mm (US
5) needles

TENSION
23 sts and 32 rows to 10cm/4in square
over St st using 3.75mm (US 5) needles,
or size to obtain correct tension.

ABBREVIATIONS
See page 63.

NOTE
When working from Chart, odd numbered
rows are knit rows and read from right
to left. Even numbered rows are purl rows
and read from left to right.
Use the Fairisle method, strand the yarn
not in use across the wrong side of work
weaving them under and over the working
yarn every 3 or 4 sts.

TO MAKE (make 2 pieces)
FIRST PIECE
Using 3.25mm needles and B, cast on 58
sts.
Beg with a k row, work in St st and
stripes of 2 rows each B, A, C, A, D, A,
E, A.
Change to 3.75mm (US 5) needles.
Work in patt from Chart.
Row 1 K2A, [work across 7-st patt rep]
8 times.

Row 2 [Work across 7-st patt rep] 8
times, p2A.
These 2 rows set Chart.
Work in patt to end of row 28.
Rep these 28 rows 7 times more, and rows
1 to 27 once more.
Leave sts on a spare needle.
SECOND PIECE
Using 3.25mm needles and B, cast on 58
sts.

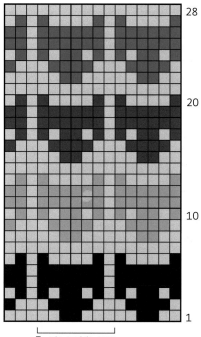

KEY
□ Scree 165 (A)
■ Bilberry 151 (B)
▨ Avocado 161 (C)
▨ Ginger 154 (D)
■ Watery 152 (E)

Beg with a k row, work
in St st and stripes of 2
rows each B, A, C, A, D,
A, E, A.
Change to 3.75mm (US 5)
needles.
Work in patt from Chart.
Row 1 K1A, [work across
7-st patt rep] 7 times,
k1A.
Row 2 P1A, [work across
7-st patt rep] 7 times,
p1A.
These 2 rows set Chart.
Work in patt to end of row
28.
Rep these 28 rows 7 times
more, and rows 1 to 20
again.
Leave sts on a spare
needle.

TO MAKE UP
With needles pointing in
the same direction, right
sides together, using A
cast off the sts of both
pieces together.
Join row ends of scarf
together.
Join cast-off edge and
cast-on edge to form a
tube.

waves slipover

FINISHED SIZE

To fit bust

81-86	91-97	102-107	cm
32-34	36-38	40-42	in

ACTUAL MEASUREMENTS

Bust

90	100	110	cm
35½	39½	43½	in

Length to shoulder

51	53	55	cm
20	21	21½	in

Longer length to shoulder

56	58	60	cm
22	23	23½	in

YARN

Rowan *Felted Tweed DK*
4(4:5) x 50g balls in Camel 157 (A)
1 x 50g ball in each of Ginger 154 (B)
and Hedgerow 187 (C)

NEEDLES

Pair each of 3.25mm (US 3) and 3.75mm (US 5) knitting needles
Stitch holders

TENSION

30 sts and 28 rows to 10cm/4in square over patterned St st of Chart A using 3.75mm (US 5) needles, or size to obtain correct tension.
23 sts and 32 rows to 10cm/4in square over patterned St st of Chart B using 3.75mm (US 5) needles, or size to obtain correct tension.

ABBREVIATIONS

See page 63.

NOTE

When working from Chart, odd numbered rows are knit rows and read from right to left. Even·numbered rows are purl rows and read from left to right.

Use the Fairisle method, strand the yarn not in use across the wrong side of work weaving them under and over the working yarn every 3 or 4 sts.

BACK

Using 3.25mm (US 3) needles and A, cast on 103(115:127) sts.
Row 1 K1, [p1, k1] to end.
Row 2 P1, [k1, p1] to end.
Rep the last 2 rows 13 times more and row 1 again.
Inc row Rib 5(11:17), m1, [rib 3, m1] 31 times, rib 5(11:17).
135(147:159) sts.
Change to 3.75mm (US 5) needles.
Cont in patt from Chart A.
Row 1 Work 2 sts before patt rep, [work across 12-st patt rep] 11(12:13) times, work one st after patt rep.
Row 2 Work one st before patt rep, [work across 12-st patt rep] 11(12:13) times, work 2 sts after patt rep.
These 2 rows set the Chart A.
Cont to work in patt from Chart A to end of row 29.
Dec row P4(10:16), p2tog, [p2, p2tog] 31 times, p5(11:17). *103(115:127) sts.*
Cont in patt from Chart B.
Row 1 Work 4 sts before patt rep, [work across 12-st patt rep] 8(9:10) times, work 3 sts after patt rep.
Row 2 Work 3 sts before patt rep, [work across 12-st patt rep] 8(9:10) times, work 4 sts after patt rep.
These 2 rows set Chart B.
Work in patt to end of row 6.
These 6 rows set the patt.
Work straight until back measures 31(32:33)cm/12(12½:13)in from cast-on edge, ending with a p row.
For longer length work 36(37:38)cm/ 14(14½:15)in from cast-on edge, ending with a p row.

SHAPE ARMHOLES

Keeping patt correct:

Cast off 9(10:11) sts at beg of next 2 rows. *85(95:105) sts.*

Next row K1, skpo, patt to last 3 sts, k2tog, k1.

Next row P1, p2tog, patt to last 3 sts, p2tog tbl, p1.

Rep the last 2 rows once more. *77(87:97) sts.*

Next row K1, skpo, patt to last 3 sts, k2tog, k1.

Next row Patt to end.

Rep the last 2 rows 3(5:7) times more. *69(75:81) sts.*

Next row K1, skpo, patt to last 3 sts, k2tog, k1.

Work 3 rows.

Next row K1, skpo, patt to last 3 sts, k2tog, k1. *65(71:77) sts.*

Work straight until back measures 49(51:53)cm/19½(20:21)in from cast-on edge, ending with a p row.

For longer length work straight until back measures 54(56:58)cm/21½(22:23)in from cast-on edge, ending with a p row.

SHAPE SHOULDERS AND BACK NECK

Cast off 5(6:7) sts at beg of next 2 rows.

Next row Cast off 5(6:7) sts, patt until there are 10 sts on the needle, turn and work on these sts for first side of neck.

Next row Cast off 4 sts, patt to end.

Cast off rem 6 sts.

With right side facing, slip centre 25(27:29) sts on a holder, rejoin yarn to rem sts, patt to end.

Next row Cast off 5(6:7) sts, patt to end.

Next row Cast off 4 sts, patt to end.

Cast off rem 6 sts.

FRONT

Work as given for Back until front is 8 rows less than back to armhole shaping, ending with a p row.

SHAPE FRONT NECK

Keeping patt correct:

Next row Patt 48(54:60), k2tog, k1, turn

CHART A

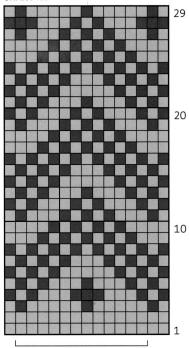

12-st patt rep

CHART B

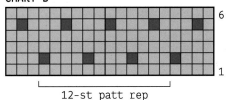

12-st patt rep

KEY

■ Camel 157 (A)
■ Ginger 154 (B)
■ Hedgerow 187 (C)

and work on these sts.

Work 3 rows.

Next row Patt to last 3 sts, k2tog, k1.

Work 3 rows.

SHAPE ARMHOLE

Next row Cast off 9(10:11) sts, patt to last 3 sts, k2tog, k1. *39(44:49) sts.*

Next row Patt to end.

Next row K1, skpo, patt to end.

Next row Patt to last 3 sts, p2tog tbl, p1.

Next row K1, skpo, patt to last 3 sts, k2tog, k1.

Next row Patt to last 3 sts, p2tog tbl, p1. *34(39:44) sts.*

Next row K1, skpo, patt to end.

Next row Patt to end.

Next row K1, skpo, patt to last 3 sts, k2tog, k1.

Next row Patt to end.

Rep the last 4 rows 1(2:3) time(s) more. *28(30:32) sts.*

Next row K1, skpo, patt to end.

Next row Patt to end.

Next row Patt to last 3 sts, k2tog, k1.

Next row Patt to end.

Next row K1, skpo, patt to end. *25(27:29) sts.*

Keeping armhole edge straight, cont to dec at neck edge on every 2nd and 4th row until 16(18:20) sts rem.

Work straight until front measures the same as back to shoulder shaping, ending at armhole edge.

SHAPE SHOULDER

Next row Cast off 5(6:7) sts at beg of next and foll right side row.

Work 1 row.

Cast off rem 6 sts.

With right side facing, place centre st on a safety pin, rejoin yarn to rem sts, k1, skpo, patt to end.

Work 3 rows.

Next row K1, skpo, patt to end.

Rep the last 4 rows once more.

SHAPE ARMHOLE

Next row Cast off 9(10:11) sts, patt to end. *39(44:49) sts.*

Next row Patt to last 3 sts, k2tog, k1.

Next row P1, p2tog, patt to end.

Next row K1, skpo, patt to last 3 sts, k2tog, k1.

Next row P1, p2tog, patt to end. *34(39:44) sts.*

Next row Patt to last 3 sts, k2tog, k1.

Next row Patt to end.

Next row K1, skpo, patt to last 3 sts, k2tog, k1.

Next row Patt to end.

Rep the last 4 rows 1(2:3) time(s) more. *28(30:32) sts.*

Next row Patt to last 3 sts, k2tog, k1.

Next row Patt to end.

Next row K1, skpo, patt to end.

Next row Patt to end.

Next row Patt to last 3 sts, k2tog, k1. *25(27:29) sts.*

Keeping armhole edge straight, cont to dec at neck edge on every 2nd and 4th row until 16(18:20) sts rem.

Work straight until front measures the same as back to shoulder shaping, ending at armhole edge.

SHAPE SHOULDER

Next row Cast off 5(6:7) sts at beg of next and foll wrong side row.

Work 1 row.

Cast off rem 6 sts.

NECKBAND

Join right shoulder seam.

With right side facing, using 3.25mm (US 3) needles and A, pick up and k56(58:60) sts down left side of front neck, k1 st from safety pin, pick up and k56(58:60) sts up right side of front neck, 8 sts down right side of back neck, k across 25(27:29) sts from back neck holder, pick up and k7 sts up left side of back neck. *153(159:165) sts.*

Next row P1, [k1, p1] to end.

This row sets the rib.

Next row Rib 54(56:58), k2tog, k1, skpo, rib to end.

Rib 1 row.
Next row Rib 53(55:57),
k2tog, k1, skpo, rib to
end.
Rib 1 row.
Next row Rib 52(54:56),
k2tog, k1, skpo, rib to
end.
Rib 1 row.
Cast off in rib,
decreasing on this row as
before.

ARMBANDS (both alike)

Join shoulder seams. Join
left shoulder and neckband
seam.
With right side facing,
using 3.25mm (US 3)
needles and A, pick up and
k123(129:135) sts evenly
round armhole edge.
Work 7 rows rib as given
for Back.
Cast off in rib.

TO MAKE UP

Join side and armband
seams.

plaid and diamond beanie

FINISHED SIZE
To fit an average-sized man's head

YARN
Rowan *Felted Tweed DK*
1 x 50g ball in each of Clay 177 (A),
Carbon 159 (B) and Cinnamon 175 (C)

NEEDLES
Pair each of 3.75mm (US 5) and 4mm
(US 6) knitting needles

TENSION
22 sts and 30 rows to 10cm/4in over St
st using 4mm (US 6) needles, or size to
obtain correct tension.

ABBREVIATIONS
See page 63.

NOTE
When working from Chart, odd numbered
rows are knit rows and read from right
to left. Even numbered rows are purl rows
and read from left to right.
Use the Fairisle method, strand the yarn
not in use across the wrong side of work
weaving them under and over the working
yarn every 3 or 4 sts.

TO MAKE
Using 3.75mm (US 5) needles and A, cast
on 138 sts.
Rib row [K1, p1] to end.
Rep the last row 9 times more.
Change to 4mm (US 6) needles and work in
patt from Chart A.
Row 1 Work first st of patt rep, then
[work 34-st patt rep] 4 times, work one
st after patt rep.
Row 2 Work first st of patt rep, then
[work 34-st patt rep] 4 times, work one
st after patt rep.

CHART A

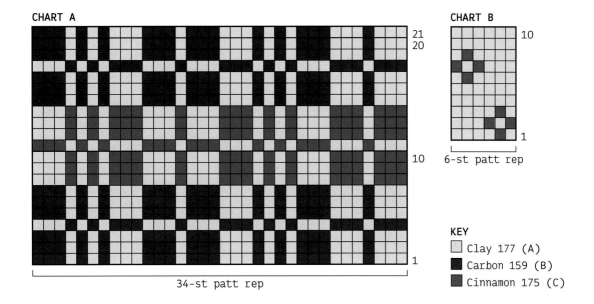

CHART B

21
20

10

1

10

1

6-st patt rep

34-st patt rep

These 2 rows set the patt.

Cont in patt to end of row 21.

Row 22 Using A, p8, p2tog, [p6, p2tog] 15 times, p8. *122 sts.*

Work in patt from Chart B.

Row 1 Work first st of patt rep, then [work 6-st patt rep] 20 times, work one st after patt rep.

Row 2 Work first st of patt rep, then [work 6-st patt rep] 20 times, work one st after patt rep.

Work from Chart until row 10.

These 10 rows set the patt.

Cont in patt until hat measures 16cm/6¼in, ending after a wrong side row.

Cont in A only.

SHAPE CROWN

Row 1 K1, [skpo, k6] 15 times, k1. *107 sts.*

Row 2 P to end.

Row 3 K1, [skpo, k5] 15 times, k1. *92 sts.*

Row 4 P to end.

Row 5 K1, [skpo, k4] 15 times, k1. *77 sts.*

Row 6 P to end.

Row 7 K1, [skpo, k3] 15 times, k1. *62 sts.*

Row 8 P to end.

Row 9 K1, [skpo, k2] 15 times, k1. *47 sts.*

Row 10 P to end.

Row 11 K1, [skpo, k1] 15 times, k1. *32 sts.*

Row 12 P to end.

Row 13 K1, [skpo] 15 times, k1. *17 sts.*

Row 14 P to end.

Row 15 K2, [skpo] 7 times, k1. *10 sts.*

Leaving a long end, cut off yarn and thread through rem sts.

TO MAKE UP

Join back seam.

plaid and diamond socks

FINISHED SIZE
To fit shoe size UK 9-10/EUR 43-44/US 10-11

YARN
Rowan *Felted Tweed DK*
2 x 50g balls in Clay 177 (A)
1 x 50g ball in each of Carbon 159 (B) and
Cinnamon 175 (C)

NEEDLES
Set of 4 double-pointed 3.75mm (US 5)
knitting needles

TENSION
23 sts and 32 rows to 10cm/4in square over
St st using 3.75mm (US 5) needles, or size
to obtain correct tension.

ABBREVIATIONS
See page 63.

NOTE
When working from Chart, all rows are knit
rows and read from right to left.
Use the Fairisle method, strand the yarn
not in use across the wrong side of work
weaving them under and over the working
yarn every 3 or 4 sts.

SOCKS (make 2)
Using 3.75mm (US 5) needles and A, cast on
54 sts.
Arrange these sts on 3 needles and cont in
rounds.
Rib round [K1, p1] to end.
Rib a further 8 rounds.
Inc round Rib 2, m1, [rib 4, m1] to end.
68 sts.
Round 1 [Work 34-st patt rep 1st row of
Chart A on page 49] twice.
This round sets the Chart.
Cont in patt to end of round 21.
Round 22 K to end, dec 2 sts evenly.
66 sts.

Work in patt from Chart B on page 49.
Round 1 [Work 6 st patt rep] 11 times.
Work from Chart until round 10.
These 10 rounds set patt.
Cont in patt until work measures
30cm/12in from cast-on edge, ending with
a plain round.
Cont in A only.
Break off yarn.
Divide sts onto 3 needles as folls: slip
first 18 sts onto first needle, next 15 sts
onto second needle and next 15 sts onto
3rd needle, slip last 18 sts onto other
end of first needle.
SHAPE HEEL
With right side facing, join yarn to 36
sts on first needle.
Work on these 36 sts only.
Working backwards and forwards in rows,
not rounds, work as folls:
Beg with a k row, work 20 rows St st.
Next row K26, skpo, turn.
Next row Sl 1, p16, p2tog, turn.
Next row Sl 1, k16, skpo, turn.
Next row Sl 1, p16, p2tog, turn.
Rep the last 2 rows 7 times more.
18 sts.
Break off yarn.
Reset sts on 3 needles as follows: slip
first 9 sts of heel sts onto a safety-
pin, place marker here to indicate beg
of round. Join A to rem sts, with first
needle k9, then pick up and 14 sts along
side of heel, with second needle k30,
with 3rd needle pick up and k14 sts along
other side of heel, k9 from safety-pin.
76 sts.
Cont in rounds.
K 1 round.
Dec round K23, k2tog, k26, k2tog tbl,
k23. *74 sts.*
K 1 round.
Dec round K22, k2tog, k26, k2tog tbl,
k22. *72 sts.*

K 1 round.
Dec round K21, k2tog, k26,
k2tog tbl, k21. *70 sts.*
K 1 round.
Dec round K20, k2tog, k26,
k2tog tbl, k20. *68 sts.*
K 1 round.
Dec round K19, k2tog, k26,
k2tog tbl, k19. *66 sts.*
K 1 round.
Dec round K18, k2tog, k26,
k2tog tbl, k18. *64 sts.*
K 1 round.
Cont in rounds of St
st until sock measures
21cm/8¼in from back of
heel.
SHAPE TOE
Next round K13, k2tog,
k2, skpo, k26, k2tog, k2,
skpo, k13. *60 sts.*
Next round K to end.
Next round K12, k2tog,
k2, skpo, k24, k2tog, k2,
skpo, k12. *56 sts.*
Next round K to end.
Next round K11, k2tog,
k2, skpo, k22, k2tog, k2,
skpo, k11. *52 sts.*
Next round K to end.
Cont in rounds decreasing
on every alt round as set
until the foll round has
been worked.
Next round K5, k2tog,
k2, skpo, k10, k2tog, k2,
skpo, k5. *28 sts.*
Slip first 7 sts onto one
needle, next 14 sts onto a
second needle, then rem 7
sts on end of first needle.
Fold sock inside out and
cast one st from each
needle off together.

soft stripe gloves

FINISHED SIZE
To fit an average-sized woman's hand

YARN
Rowan *Felted Tweed DK*
2 x 50g balls in Clay 177 (A)
1 x 50g ball in each of Gilt 160 (B),
Seasalter 178 (C), Duck Egg 173 (D) and
Celadon 184 (E)

NEEDLES
Pair each of 3.25mm (US 3) and 3.75mm
(US 5) knitting needles

TENSION
23 sts and 32 rows to 10cm/4in square
over St st using 3.75mm (US 5) needles,
or size to obtain correct tension.

ABBREVIATIONS
See page 63.

NOTE
When working from Chart, odd numbered
rows are knit rows and read from right
to left. Even numbered rows are purl rows
and read from left to right.
Use the Fairisle method, strand the yarn
not in use across the wrong side of work
weaving them under and over the working
yarn every 3 or 4 sts.

RIGHT GLOVE
** Using 3.25mm (US 3) needles and A,
cast on 52 sts.
Rib row [K1, p1] to end.
* Rep the last row twice more, dec one st
at centre of last row. *51 sts.*
Change to 3.75mm needles and work in St
st and patt from Chart.
Row 1 Work 2 sts before patt rep, then
[work 6-st patt rep] 8 times, work one st
after patt rep.
Row 2 Work one st before patt rep, then
[work 6-st patt rep] 8 times, work 2 sts
after patt rep.
These 2 rows set the patt.
Cont in patt to end of row 17, dec one st
at centre of last row. *50 sts.*
Row 18 Using A, p to end.
Row 19 Using A, k to end.
Row 20 Using A, k to end to mark hemline.
Change to 3.25mm (US 3) needles.
Beg with a p row, cont in St st and
stripes of 2 rows A, then 3 rows E and 3
rows A.
Work a further 17 rows, ending with a p
row.
Change to 3.75mm (US 5) needles.
Work a further 12 rows **.
THUMB SHAPING
Next row K25, m1, k3, m1, k to end.
Work 3 rows.
Next row K25, m1, k5, m1, k to end.
Work 1 row.
Next row K25, m1, k7, m1, k to end.
Work 1 row.
Next row K25, m1, k9, m1, k to end.
Work 1 row. *58 sts.*
Cont to inc as set on every right side
row until there are 64 sts on needle.
Work 1 row.
Divide for thumb
Next row K42, turn.
Next row P17, turn.
Cont in A only.
Work 16 rows in St st.
Next row K1, [k2tog] to end. *9 sts.*
Break yarn, thread through rem sts, draw
up tightly and join seam.
With RS facing, join yarn to base of
thumb, k to end. *47 sts.*
Work 15 rows.
Cont in A only.
*** **Divide for fingers**
FIRST FINGER
Next row K30, turn and cast on 2 sts.
Next row P15, turn.

Work 20 rows in St st.
Next row K1, [k2tog] to end. *8 sts.*
Break yarn, thread through rem sts, draw
up tightly and join seam.
SECOND FINGER
With RS facing, join yarn to base of first
finger, pick up and k2 sts from base of
first finger, k6, turn, cast on 2 sts.
Next row P16, turn.
Work 24 rows in St st.
Next row [K2tog] to end. *8 sts.*
Break yarn, thread through rem sts, draw
up tightly and join seam.
THIRD FINGER
With RS facing, join yarn to base of
second finger, pick up and k2 sts from
base of second finger, k6, turn, cast on
2 sts.
Next row P16, turn.
Work 20 rows in St st.
Next row [K2tog] to end. *8 sts.*
Break yarn, thread through rem sts, draw
up tightly and join seam.
FOURTH FINGER
With RS facing, join yarn to base of
third finger, pick up and k2 sts from base
of third finger, k5, turn.
Next row P12.
Work 14 rows in St st.
Next row [K2tog] to end. *6 sts.*
Break yarn thread through rem sts, draw
up tightly and join seam.

LEFT GLOVE
Work as given for Right Glove from ** to
**.
THUMB SHAPING
Next row K22, m1, k3, m1, k to end.
Work 3 rows.
Next row K22, m1, k5, m1, k to end.
Work 1 row.
Next row K22, m1, k7, m1, k to end.
Work 1 row.
Next row K22, m1, k9, m1, k to end.
Work 1 row.
Cont to inc as set on every right side
row until there are 64 sts on needle.

Work 1 row.
Divide for thumb
Next row K39, turn.
Next row P17 sts, turn.
Cont in A only.
Work 16 rows in St st.
Next row K1, [k2tog] to end. *9 sts.*
Break yarn, thread through rem sts, draw
up tightly and join seam.
With RS facing, join yarn in correct
colour to base of thumb, k to end.
47 sts.
Work 15 rows.
Cont in A only.
Complete as for Right Glove from *** to
end.

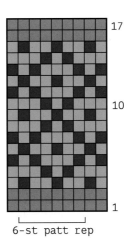

6-st patt rep

KEY
■ Gilt 160 (B)
■ Seasalter 178 (C)
■ Duck Egg 173 (D)

soft stripe beret

FINISHED SIZE
To fit an average-sized woman's head

YARN
Rowan *Felted Tweed DK*
1 x 50g ball in each of Clay 177 (A),
Gilt 160 (B) Seasalter 178 (C), Duck Egg
173 (D) and Celadon 184 (E)

NEEDLES
Pair each of 3.75mm (US 5) and 4mm
(US 6) knitting needles

TENSION
22 sts and 30 rows to 10cm/4in over
patterned St st using 4mm (US 6) needles,
or size to obtain correct tension.

ABBREVIATIONS
See page 63.

TO MAKE
Using 3.75mm (US 5) needles and A, cast
on 111 sts.
Rib row 1 K1, [p1, k1] to end.
Rib row 2 P1, [k1, p1] to end.
Rep the last 2 rows twice more and the
first row again.
Inc row (WS) Rib 3, [m1, rib 3] to end.
147 sts.
Change to 4mm (US 6) needles and work in
St st and patt from Chart on page 53.
Row 1 Work 2 sts before patt rep, then
[work 6-st patt rep] 24 times, work one
st after patt rep.
Row 2 Work first st before patt rep, then
[work 6-st patt rep] 24 times, work 2 sts
after patt rep.
These 2 rows set the patt.
Cont in patt to end of row 17.
Cont in St st and stripes of 3 rows A and
3 rows E as folls:
Row 18 Using A, p to end, dec one st at
centre of row. *146 sts.*

Work 30 rows.

SHAPE CROWN
Row 1 K1, [skpo, k10] 12 times, k1.
134 sts.
Row 2 P to end.
Row 3 K1, [skpo, k9] 12 times, k1.
122 sts.
Row 4 P to end.
Row 5 K1, [skpo, k8] 12 times, k1.
110 sts.
Row 6 P to end.
Row 7 K1, [skpo, k7] 12 times, k1.
98 sts.
Row 8 P to end.
Row 9 K1, [skpo, k6] 12 times, k1.
86 sts.
Row 10 P to end.
Row 11 K1, [skpo, k5] 12 times, k1.
74 sts.
Row 12 P to end.
Row 13 K1, [skpo, k4] 12 times, k1.
62 sts.
Row 14 P to end.
Row 15 K1, [skpo, k3] 12 times, k1.
50 sts.
Row 16 P to end.
Row 17 K1, [skpo, k2] 12 times, k1.
38 sts.
Row 18 P to end.
Row 19 K1, [skpo, k1] 12 times, k1.
26 sts.
Row 20 P1, [p2tog] 12 times, p1. *14 sts.*
Row 21 K1, [skpo] 6 times, k1. *8 sts.*
Leaving a long end, cut off yarn and
thread through rem sts.

TO MAKE UP
Join seam.

nordic throw

FINISHED SIZE
Approx 79cm/31in by 107cm/42in

YARN
Rowan *Felted Tweed DK*
Approx 500g of assorted colours,
including Phantom 153 (A) for trunk.
Each large square requires approx 12g
of main colour (MC).
We used 2 x 50g balls of Mineral 181,
for spots (CC) and edgings.

NEEDLES
Pair each of 2.75mm (US 2) and 3.75mm
(US 5) knitting needles
3.25mm (US 3) circular needle

TENSION
23 sts and 32 rows to 10cm/4in square
over St st using 3.75mm (US 5) needles,
or size to obtain correct tension.

ABBREVIATIONS
See page 63.

NOTE
When working from Chart, odd numbered
rows are knit rows and read from right
to left. Even numbered rows are purl rows
and read from left to right.
Use the Fairisle method, strand the yarn
not in use across the wrong side of work
weaving them under and over the working
yarn every 3 or 4 sts.
You will need to make 35 motifs for the
Throw shown.

PLAIN SQUARES
Leaving a long end of approx 30cm/12in,
using 3.75mm (US 5) needles and colour of
choice, cast on 37 sts.
Beg with a k row, work 44 rows in St st.
Cast off.

BIRD'S EYE SQUARE
Leaving a long end of approx 30cm/12in,
using 3.75mm (US 5) needles and colour of
choice (MC), cast on 37 sts.
Row 1 K to end.
Row 2 P to end.
Row 3 K4MC, [1CC, 3MC] to last 5 sts, 1CC,
4MC.
Row 4 P to end.
Row 5 K to end.
Row 6 P2MC, [1CC, 3MC] to last 3 sts, 1CC,
2MC.
These 6 rows form the patt.
Work a further 38 rows, ending row 2.
Leaving a long end of approx 30cm/12in,
cast off.

GARTER ST NORDIC TREE
TRUNK
Leaving a long end of approx 20cm/8in,
using 2.75mm (US 2) needles and A, cast
on 5 sts.
K 10 rows.
Leave these sts on a spare needle.
MAIN PART
Leaving a long end of approx 30cm/12in,
using 2.75mm (US 2) needles and colour of
choice (MC), cast on 15 sts.
Row 1 (RS) K5, with wrong side of trunk
to right side of work, [k1tog with one st
from trunk] 5 times, k5.
Row 2 K to end.
Row 3 Skpo, k to last 2 sts, k2tog. *13 sts.*
K 3 rows.
Rep the last 4 rows 5 times more. *3 sts.*
K3tog and leaving a long end, fasten off.

FAIRISLE NORDIC TREE
TRUNK
Leaving a long end of approx 20cm/8in,
using 2.75mm (US 2) needles and A, cast on
7 sts.
K 10 rows.
Leave these sts on a spare needle.

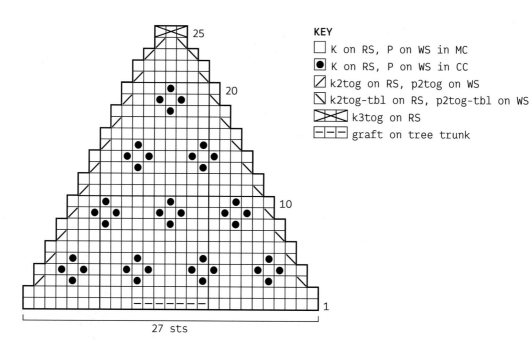

KEY
☐ K on RS, P on WS in MC
▣ K on RS, P on WS in CC
◪ k2tog on RS, p2tog on WS
◩ k2tog-tbl on RS, p2tog-tbl on WS
⬚⬚ k3tog on RS
⊟⊟⊟ graft on tree trunk

25

20

10

1

27 sts

MAIN PART

We created different size trees by using either 2.75mm (US 2) needles or 3.75mm (US 5) needles.
Leaving a long end of approx 30cm/12in, using 2.75mm (US 2) or 3.75mm (US 5) needles and colour of choice (MC), cast on 27 sts.
Row 1 K10, with right side of trunk to wrong side of cast on row, [k1tog with 1 st from trunk] 7 times, k10.
Row 2 P to end.
Work in patt from row 3 of Chart, shaping as shown.

TOP EDGING

Sew trees to squares.
Join squares together to form a rectangle 5 squares wide by 7 squares deep and alternating motifs.
With right side facing, using 3.25mm (US 3) circular needle, pick up and k177 sts along cast-off edge.
Next row K to end.

Next row K1, m1, k to last st, m1, k1. *179 sts.*
Rep the last 2 rows twice more. *183 sts.*
Cast off.

BOTTOM EDGING

With right side facing, using 3.25mm (US 3) circular needle, pick up and k177 sts along cast-on edge.
Work as given for top edging.

SIDE EDGINGS (both alike)

With right side facing, using circular needle, pick up and k196 sts along side edges.
Next row K to end.
Next row K1, m1, k to last st, m1, k1. *198 sts.*
Rep the last 2 rows twice more. *202 sts.*
Cast off.

TO MAKE UP

Join corners of edgings.

nordic cushion

FINISHED SIZE
28cm/11in by 28cm/11in to fit a 30cm/12in square cushion pad.

YARN
Rowan *Felted Tweed DK*
One x 50g ball in each of Avocado 161 (A) and Rage 150 (B)
Approx 20g of Mineral 181 (C)
Small amount of Phantom 153 (D) and Seasalter 178 (E)
You will need approx 150g of assorted colours altogether

NEEDLES
Pair each of 2.75mm (US 2) and 3.75mm (US 5) knitting needles

EXTRAS
30cm/12in square cushion pad

TENSION
23 sts and 32 rows to 10cm/4in square over St st using 3.75mm (US 5) needles, or size to obtain correct tension.

ABBREVIATIONS
See page 63.

NOTE
When working from Chart, odd numbered rows are knit rows and read from right to left. Even numbered rows are purl rows and read from left to right.
Use the Fairisle method, strand the yarn not in use across the wrong side of work weaving them under and over the working yarn every 3 or 4 sts.

PLAIN SQUARE (make 2)
Leaving a long end of approx 30cm/12in, using 3.75mm (US 5) needles and A, cast on 37 sts.
Beg with a k row, work 44 rows in St st.
Leaving a long end of approx 30cm/12in, cast off.

BIRD'S EYE SQUARE (make 2)
Leaving a long end of approx 30cm/12in, using 3.75mm (US 5) needles and B, cast on 37 sts.
Row 1 Using B, k to end.
Row 2 P to end.
Row 3 K4B, [1C, 3B] to last 5 sts, 1C, 4B.
Row 4 Using B, p to end.
Row 5 K to end.
Row 6 P2M, [1C, 3M] to last 3 sts, 1C, 2M.
These 6 rows form the patt.
Work a further 38 rows, ending row 2.
Leaving a long end of approx 30cm/12in, cast off.

GARTER ST NORDIC TREE
(make 2)
TRUNK
Leaving a long end of approx 20cm/8in, using 2.75mm (US 2) needles and D, cast on 5 sts.
K 10 rows.
Leave these sts on a spare needle.
MAIN PART
Leaving a long end of approx 30cm/12in, using 2.75mm (US 2) needles and E, cast on 15 sts.
Row 1 (RS) K5, with right side of trunk to wrong side of cast-on row, [k1tog with one st from trunk] 5 times, k5.
Row 2 K to end.
Row 3 Skpo, k to last 2 sts, k2tog.
13 sts.
K 3 rows.
Rep the last 4 rows 5 times more. *3 sts.*
K3tog and leaving a long end, fasten off.

FAIRISLE NORDIC TREE
(make 2)

TRUNK

Leaving a long end of approx 20cm/8in, using 2.75mm (US 2) needles and D, cast on 7 sts.

K 10 rows.

Leave these sts on a spare needle.

MAIN PART

Leaving a long end of approx 30cm/12in, using 2.75mm (US 2) needles and B, cast on 27 sts.

Row 1 K10, with right side of trunk to wrong side of cast-on row, [k1tog with one st from trunk] 7 times, k10.

Row 2 P to end.

Work in patt from row 3 of Chart, shaping as shown.

BACK

Using 3.75mm (US 5) needles and colour of choice (we used B), cast on 71 sts.

Work 88 rows in 4 row stripes in colours of choice.

Cast off.

TO MAKE UP

Sew trees to squares. Join squares to form the front.

With right sides together, sew back to front along 3 sides. Insert cushion pad, join rem side.

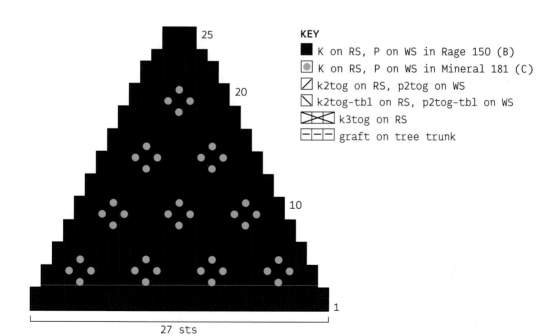

KEY

- ■ K on RS, P on WS in Rage 150 (B)
- ◉ K on RS, P on WS in Mineral 181 (C)
- ◩ k2tog on RS, p2tog on WS
- ◪ k2tog-tbl on RS, p2tog-tbl on WS
- ⬚ k3tog on RS
- −−− graft on tree trunk

27 sts

nordic garland

FINISHED SIZE
165cm/64in long

YARN
Rowan *Felted Tweed DK*
Small amount of Phantom 153 (A) for trunk
Oddments in an assortment of colours for tree (MC) and pattern (CC)
Approx 20g of one colour for i-cord

NEEDLES
Two double-pointed 2.75mm (US 2) knitting needles

EXTRAS
15 assorted buttons

ABBREVIATIONS
See page 63.

NOTE
When working from Chart, odd numbered rows are knit rows and read from right to left. Even numbered rows are purl rows and read from left to right.
Use the Fairisle method, strand the yarn not in use across the wrong side of work weaving them under and over the working yarn every 2 or 3 sts.

GARTER ST NORDIC TREE
TRUNK
Using 2.75mm (US 2) needles and A, cast on 5 sts.
K10 rows.
Leave these sts on a spare needle.
MAIN PART
Using 2.75mm (US 2) needles, cast on 15 sts.
Row 1 (RS) K5, with wrong side of trunk to right side of work, [k1tog with one st from trunk] 5 times, k5.
Row 2 K to end.
Row 3 Skpo, k to last 2 sts, k2tog.

13 sts.
K 3 rows.
Rep the last 4 rows 5 times more. *3 sts.*
K3tog and leaving a long end, fasten off.

FAIRISLE NORDIC TREE A
TRUNK
Using 2.75mm (US 2) needles and A, cast on 5 sts.
K 10 rows.
Leave these sts on a spare needle.
MAIN PART
Using 2.75mm (US 2) needles and MC, cast on 23 sts.
Row 1 (RS) K9, with wrong side of trunk to right side of work, [k1tog with one st from trunk] 5 times, k9.
Row 2 P to end.
Work in patt from row 3 of Chart A, shaping as shown.

FAIRISLE NORDIC TREE B
TRUNK
Using 2.75mm (US 2) needles and A, cast on 7 sts.
K 10 rows.
Leave these sts on a spare needle.
MAIN PART
Using 2.75mm (US 2) needles and MC, cast on 27 sts.
Row 1 (RS) K10, with wrong side of trunk to right side of work, [k1tog with one st from trunk] 7 times, k10.
Row 2 P to end.
Work in patt from row 3 of Chart B, shaping as shown.

I-CORD
Using 2.75mm (US 2) needles, cast on 4 sts.
*K4, do not turn, slide sts back to other end of needle, bring yarn tightly across back of work; rep from * until i-cord measures 165cm/65in from beg. Cast off.

TO MAKE UP

Arrange trees along i-cord 11cm/4¼in apart and secure top of tree to i-cord with a button.

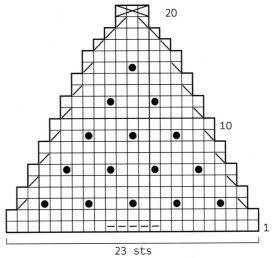

CHART A (Fairisle Nordic Tree A)

23 sts

KEY

- ☐ K on RS, P on WS in MC
- ● K on RS, P on WS in CC
- ◿ k2tog on RS, p2tog on WS
- ◺ k2tog-tbl on RS, p2tog-tbl on WS
- ⊠ k3tog on RS
- ⊟⊟ graft on tree trunk

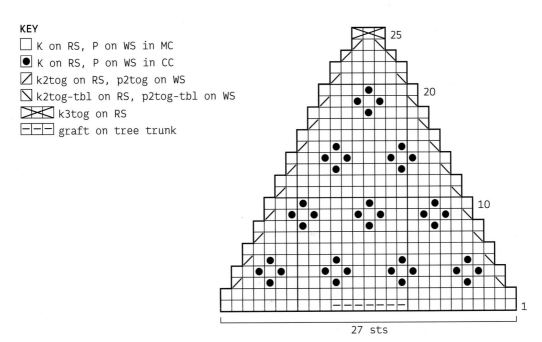

CHART B (Fairisle Nordic Tree B)

27 sts

useful information

FAIRISLE

When you are working a pattern with two (or more) repeating colours in the same row, you need to strand the yarn not in use behind the stitches being worked. This needs to be done with care, loosely enough to ensure that the strands not in work do not tighten and pucker the front of the knitting. To do this you need to treat the yarns not in use (known as floating yarns) as if they were one yarn and spreads the stitches as you work to their correct width to keep them elastic. If your pattern demands that the stranded (floating) yarns are carried across more than three stitches, it is wise each time you change colours to weave the new yarn colour under and over the colour yarn you are working (over the first time, under the second time and so on). The alternating 'under and over' movement helps to prevent the floating yarns from tangling by keeping them caught at the back of the work. If you tend to knit colourwork too tightly, increase your needle size for the colourwork section. If you make a minor mistake using the Fairisle technique – say, just a single stitch – you can recreate it in the correct colour using the Swiss darning technique, in which you duplicate the stitch using a darning needle and the chosen colour.

TENSION

To check your tension, knit a square in the pattern stitch and/or stocking stitch of perhaps 5-10 more stitches and 5-10 more rows than those given in the tension note. Press the finished square under a damp cloth and mark out the central 10cm/4in square with pins. If you have too many stitches to 10cm/4in, try again using thicker needles. If you have too few stitches to 10cm/4in, try again using finer needles.

CHART NOTES

Each square of the chart represents a stitch and each line of squares represents a row of knitting. When working from charts, read odd-numbered rows (K) from right to left and even numbered rows (P) from left to right, unless otherwise stated.

FINISHING METHODS
Pressing

Block out each piece of knitting by pinning it on a board to the correct measurements in the pattern. Then lightly press it according to the ball band instructions, omitting any ribbed areas. Take special care to press the edges as this makes sewing up easier and neater. Darn in all ends neatly along the selvedge edge or a colour join, as appropriate.

Stitching seams

When you stitch the pieces together, remember to match any areas of colour and texture carefully where they meet. After all the seams are complete, press the seams and hems.

ROWAN *FELTED TWEED DK*

A wool-alpaca-viscose mix (50 per cent merino wool, 25 per cent alpaca wool, 25 per cent viscose); 50g (approx 175m/191yd) per ball. Recommended tension: 22-24 sts and 30-32 rows to 10cm/4in in St st using 3.5-4mm (US size 5-6) knitting needles.

acknowledgments

ABBREVIATIONS
The knitting pattern abbreviations used in this book are as below.

alt	alternate
approx	approximately
beg	begin(s)(ning)
cm	centimetres
cont	continu(e)(ing)
CC	contrast colour
dec	decreas(e)(ing)
DPN	double-pointed needle
foll(s)	follow(s)(ing)
g	gram
in	inch(es)
inc	increas(e)(ing)
k	knit
k2tog	knit next 2 sts together
MC	main colour
mm	millimetres
m1	make one st by picking up horizontal loop before next st and knitting into back of it
p	purl
patt	pattern
p2tog	purl next 2 sts together
rem	remain(s)(ing)
rep	repeat
rev St st	reverse stocking stitch
RS	right side
skpo	sl 1, k1, pass slipped stitch over
sl 1	slip one st
sl 1pw	slip one st purlwise
st(s)	stitch(es)
St st	stocking stitch (1 row knit, 1 row purl)
tbl	through back of loop(s)
tog	together
WS	wrong side
yd	yard(s)
[ ]/*	repeat instructions within square brackets or between asterisks

A big, big thank you to the following team of people: Steven and Susan for their great work on photography, art direction and styling; my niece, Harriet, for modelling so beautifully; Anne, for her gorgeous page layouts; our fabulous pattern writer, Penny Hill and her band of wonderful knitters; Frances, for the beautifully knitted swatches; Katie and Jill for their diligent editing and checking; and the entire Rowan team for their continuous support.

PUBLISHERS' ACKNOWLEDGMENTS
All this was made easy by working with a consummate professional like Martin! Many, many thanks to him and to the 'team' for their similar professional ethic.

stockists

U.K.
Rowan, Green Lane Mill,
Holmfirth,
West Yorkshire HD9 2DX
www.knitrowan.com

U.S.A.
Westminster Fibers Inc,
8 Shelter Drive, Greer
South Carolina 29650
www.westminsterfibers.com

AUSTRALIA
Australian Country Spinners
Pty Ltd,
Melbourne, Victoria 3004
tkohut@auspinners.com.au

AUSTRIA
Coats Harlander Ges GmbH
1210 Vienna
www.coatscrafts.at

BELGIUM
See Germany

BULGARIA
Coats Bulgaria
BG-1784 Sofia
www.coatsbulgaria.bg

CANADA
Westminster Fibers Inc,
Vaughan, Ontario L4H 3M8
www.westminsterfibers.coom

CHINA
Coats Shanghai Ltd, Shanghai
victor.li@coats.com

CYPRUS
See Bulgaria

DENMARK
Coats Expotex AB, Dalsjöfors
info.dk@coats.com

FINLAND
Coats Opti Crafts Oy, Kerava
04200
www.coatscrafts.fi

FRANCE
www.coatscrafts.fr

GERMANY
Coats GmbH, Kenzingen 79341
www.coatsgmbh.de

GREECE
See Bulgaria

HONG KONG
East Unity Company Ltd,
Chai Wan
eastunityco@yahoo.com.hk

ICELAND
Rowan At Storkurinn,
Reykjavik 101
www.storkurinn.is

ITALY
Coats Cucirini srl, Milan
20126
www.coatscucirini.com

KOREA
Coats Korea Co. Lt,
Seoul 137-060
www.coatskorea.co.kr

LEBANON
y.knot, Saifi Village, Beirut
y.knot@cyberia.net.lb

LITHUANIA & RUSSIA
Coats Lietuva UAB,
Vilnius 09310
www.coatscrafts.lt

LUXEMBOURG
See Germany

NEW ZEALAND
ACS New Zealand,
Christchurch
64 3 323 6665

NORWAY
Coats Knappehuset AS,
Bergen 5873
kundeservice@coats.com

PORTUGAL
Coats & Clark,
Vila Nova de Gaia 4400
351 223 770700

SINGAPORE
Golden Dragon Store,
Singapore 058357
gdscraft@hotmail.com

SOUTH AFRICA
Arthur Bales Ltd,
Johannesburg 2195
arthurb@new.co.za

SPAIN
Coats Fabra,
Barcelona 08030
www.coatscrafts.es

SWEDEN
Coats Expotex AB
kundtjanst@coats.com

SWITZERLAND
Coats Stroppel AG,
Untersiggenthal 5417
www.coatscrafts.ch

TAIWAN
Cactus Quality Co Ltd,
Taiwan, R.O.C. 10084
00886-2-23656527

THAILAND
Global Wide Trading,
Bangkok 10310
global.wide@yahoo.com

For stockists in all other
countries please contact
Rowan for details